DATE DUE

FIRST SCIENCE

Temperature

by Kay Manolis

°C

3.1

°F

Consultant:
Duane Quam, M.S. Physics
Chair, Minnesota State
Academic Science Standards
Writing Committee

BLASTOFF!
READERS
4

BELLWETHER MEDIA • MINNEAPOLIS, MN

Note to Librarians, Teachers, and Parents:

Blastoff! Readers are carefully developed by literacy experts and combine standards-based content with developmentally-appropriate text.

Level 1 provides the most support through repetition of high-frequency words, light text, predictable sentence patterns, and strong visual support.

Level 2 offers early readers a bit more challenge through varied simple sentences, increased text load, and less repetition of high frequency words.

Level 3 advances early-fluent readers toward fluency through increased text and concept load, less reliance on visuals, longer sentences, and more literary language.

Level 4 builds reading stamina by providing more text per page, increased use of punctuation, greater variation in sentence patterns, and increasingly challenging vocabulary.

Level 5 encourages children to move from "learning to read" to "reading to learn" by providing even more text, varied writing styles, and less familiar topics.

Whichever book is right for your reader, Blastoff! Readers are the perfect books to build confidence and encourage a love of reading that will last a lifetime!

This edition first published in 2008 by Bellwether Media.

No part of this publication may be reproduced in whole or in part without written permission of the publisher. For information regarding permission, write to Bellwether Media Inc., Attention: Permissions Department, Post Office Box 1C, Minnetonka, MN 55345-9998.

Library of Congress Cataloging-in-Publication Data
Manolis, Kay.
  Temperature / by Kay Manolis.
    p. cm. – (Blastoff! readers. First science)
Summary: "First Science explains introductory physical science concepts about temperature through real-world observation and simple scientific diagrams. Intended for students in grades three through six"—Provided by publisher.
  Includes bibliographical references and index.
  ISBN-13: 978-1-60014-100-3 (hardcover : alk. paper)
  ISBN-10: 1-60014-100-5 (hardcover : alk. paper)
  1. Temperature–Juvenile literature. 2. Temperature measurements–Juvenile literature. I. Title.

QC271.4.M36 2008
536'.5–dc22   2007021129

Contents

Hot and Cold

Everyone knows how something feels when it is hot. A sandy beach on a summer afternoon can feel hot. Pizza fresh from the oven can feel very hot!

Everyone knows how something cold feels too. An icy glass of lemonade feels cold. A snowball feels cold. The wind in winter can feel very cold!

Temperature is a measure of how hot or how cold things are. Hot things, such as fire or the oven, have higher temperatures. Cold things, such as snow or popsicles, have lower temperatures.

Often, you can tell whether an object's temperature is hot or cold without even touching it. Hot things make the air around them feel hot. Cold things make the air around them feel cold.

Measuring Temperature

A **thermometer** is a tool
that measures temperature
in units called **degrees**.
More degrees mean
higher temperatures.
Fewer degrees mean
lower temperatures.
Thermometers may use a
Fahrenheit scale or a
Celsius scale. They may
also use both scales.

fun fact

The lowest recorded
temperature on Earth is
-128.56°F (-89.2°C) at the
Vostok Station in Antarctica
on July 21, 1983.

Hot and cold temperatures can be helpful.
Cold temperatures inside your refrigerator
keep your food fresh.

Hot temperatures inside your oven let you bake food such as bread or cookies. Controls on the outside of the oven let you set the right temperature for the food you are baking.

Most of the time, your body's temperature stays about the same. It goes up when you get sick. A high temperature is called a **fever**. Fevers help your body get healthy.

Knowing the temperature is helpful. You wear a coat if you know the temperature outside is low. You wear lighter clothing when the temperature outside is high.

The Effects of Temperature

Temperature affects the weather. Air sinks when it has a low temperature. Air rises when it is warmed by the sun. Thunderstorms occur when hot, wet air meets cold, dry air. When air temperatures fall low enough, rain can change to snow or ice.

! fun fact

The highest recorded temperature on Earth is 136°F (58°C). It was recorded in Tripoli, Libya, on September 13th, 1922.

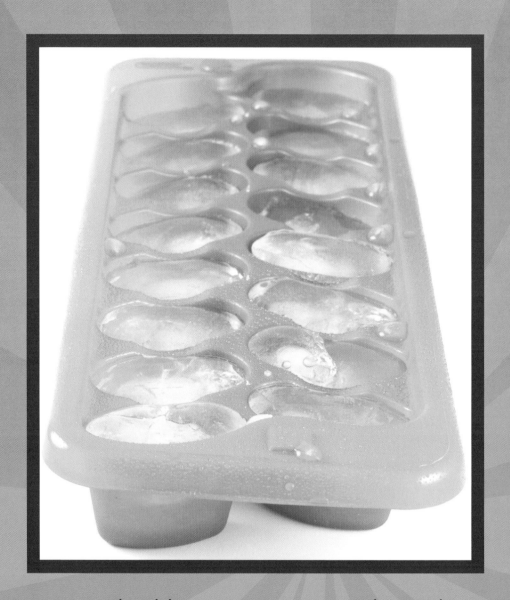

Hot and cold temperatures can also make things change. What happens if you place a tray of water in the freezer where the temperature is very cold? The water will turn into ice.

What happens if you place water over heat? It **boils** when it reaches a certain temperature. Always be careful around boiling water! It is very, very hot.

Hot temperatures can make things burn. Paper or wood can burn if they get hot enough. Food will burn if it gets too hot in your oven.

Hot temperatures can also melt things. Ice cream melts quickly in the hot temperatures of summer!

Your body has ways to keep a steady temperature. When you are hot, your body makes a liquid called **sweat** to help you cool down. Jumping in a pool or drinking a glass of cold water can also help you feel cooler. When you are cold, your body can **shiver** to warm you up. You can also wrap yourself in blankets to keep warm during winter!

fun fact

Heat is made whenever two things rub together. Try rubbing your two hands together. Soon you will feel them warming up.

Glossary

boil—to heat a liquid until it begins turning into a gas

Celsius—a system for measuring temperature; the Celsius system is used in most countries around the world.

degrees—units of temperature

Fahrenheit—a system for measuring temperature; the Fahrenheit system is used in the United States.

fever—a higher than normal body temperature

shiver—when the body shakes to warm itself up

sweat—the liquid your body produces to cool you down when you are hot

thermometer—a tool for measuring temperature

To Learn More

AT THE LIBRARY

Auch, Alison. *That's Hot!* Minneapolis, Minn.: Compass Point, 2002.

Gardner, Robert. *Really Hot Science Projects With Temperature: How Hot Is It? How Cold Is It?* New York: Enslow, 2003.

Maestro, Betsy and Giulio Maestro. *Temperature and You*. New York: Dutton, 1990.

ON THE WEB

Learning more about temperature is as easy as 1, 2, 3.

1. Go to www.factsurfer.com

2. Enter "temperature" into search box.

3. Click the "Surf" button and you will see a list of related web sites.

With factsurfer.com, finding more information is just a click away.

Index

The images in this book are reproduced through the courtesy of: Christopher Hudson, front cover; Donald Swartz, p. 4; Olga Lyubkina, p. 5; Yellow Dog Productions/Getty Images, pp. 6, 13; Studio MPM/Getty Images, p. 7; EUToch, pp. 8-9; Ray Pietro/Getty Images, p. 10; mauritius images/agefotostock, p. 11; Arthur Tilley/Getty Images, p. 12; Sander van de Wijngaert, pp. 14-15; Karamala/dreamstime, p. 16; Jonathan Borzicchi, p. 17; Melissa Dockstader, p. 18; Lori Sparkla, p. 19; Stavchansky Yakov, pp. 20-21.